Medieval Africa for Kids

A Captivating Guide to Mansa Musa, the Mali Empire, and other African Civilizations of the Middle Ages

Table of Contents

Introduction   1

Chapter 1: The African Middle Ages   2

Chapter 2: The Ghana Empire   10

Chapter 3: The Kanem-Bornu Empire   17

Chapter 4: The Kingdom of Benin   24

Chapter 5: The Mali Empire   31

Chapter 6: Emperor Mansa Musa   39

Chapter 7: The Kingdom of Abyssiania   46

Chapter 8: The Songhay Kingdom   53

Chapter 9: Society and Famous Rulers   59

Chapter 10: Culture and Art   66

Answer Key   73

If you want to learn more about tons of other

exciting historical periods, check out our other books!   77

Bibliography   78

INTRODUCTION

You've probably heard about the Middle Ages. It was the time after the Roman Empire when Europe struggled to rebuild. There were knights and kings, and the Vikings attacked many towns across Europe.

When most of us think about the medieval era, we think about Europe. But have you ever wondered what the Middle Ages were like in other places? Medieval Africa was very different from Europe—in fact, it was much more powerful! Many empires ruled in Africa during this time, and they became wealthy due to trade. Africa had many natural resources, like salt and gold. Merchants traveled across the ocean and the Sahara Desert to trade with the African people. Many of these merchants were Muslims. During medieval Africa's history, Islam became an important part of daily life, but the African people did not just blindly accept a new religion. Instead, they took Islam, combined it with their traditional religions, and made something unique. Medieval Africa was full of creativity, innovation, scholarship, and riches that made the whole world take notice.

But how did medieval Africa make these trade connections? What did they do with all their wealth? How many empires were there, and how long were they powerful? Medieval Africa is full of questions like these.

Children and parents will enjoy reading this fun, up-to-date history of this long-forgotten area of medieval history. This book has everything you need to learn about the empires, rulers, and innovations that made medieval Africa powerful. Get ready to set off across history to discover cities of gold and the people who called Africa home.

Chapter 1: The African Middle Ages

When we think about the **Middle Ages**, most people think about Europe. The Middle Ages in Europe were hard and full of chaos. The people were trying to rebuild their lives after the fall of the Roman Empire, and that took a lot of time.

However, other places also had a medieval period, and they thrived! Instead of confusion and chaos, it was a time of growth and new discoveries. One of those places was **Africa.**

Historians study African history differently than history from other continents. We don't have many written documents from ancient or medieval Africa, even though there were many powerful kingdoms that impacted the world. Most of the written texts we have come from empires outside of Africa.

Fun Fact: A few African kingdoms, like Ethiopia, wrote a lot during the Middle Ages.

Of course, that doesn't mean that medieval Africa wasn't full of new discoveries and incredible art. In fact, much of the information we have about these kingdoms comes from **archeology**. The kingdoms left behind buildings and other objects that tell us a lot about their cultures, and historians use them to piece together medieval African history.

COOL FACT: Historians also use rock art and oral traditions to understand the Middle Ages in Africa. Oral traditions are stories that have been told many times over many generations.

This history was full of rich kingdoms and vibrant cultures. There were many different kingdoms.

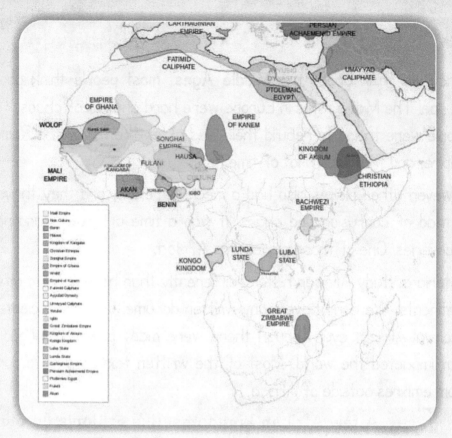

Map of Ancient & Medieval Sub-Saharan African States
Jeff Israel (ZyMOS), CC BY-SA 3.0 <https://creativecommons.org/licenses/by-sa/3.0>,
via Wikimedia Commons https://commons.wikimedia.org/wiki/File:African-civilizations-map-pre-colonial.svg

Most historians say the Middle Ages lasted from about 500 CE to 1500 CE. That's about a thousand years! Africa was very diverse, and a lot happened on the continent. Many of the kingdoms were powerful and rich.

One of the events that impacted the African Middle Ages was the spread of **Islam**. Islam is a world religion that believes in **God**. It started in the Middle East, but it has now spread all over the world. Muslims believe that God spoke to the prophet **Muhammad** and gave him new laws.

These new rules focus on **justice** and living in the right way. By the mid-600s, Islam had already spread to parts of northern Africa—and would continue to expand from there. You might think Islam spread across Africa in an orderly manner that is easy to follow. However, it is a little more complicated. Islam spread into Africa in several different areas, but it took a very long time to reach the whole continent. Towns and empires on the coast were first to adopt the religion. Sometimes, they even adapted it by adding their own traditions.

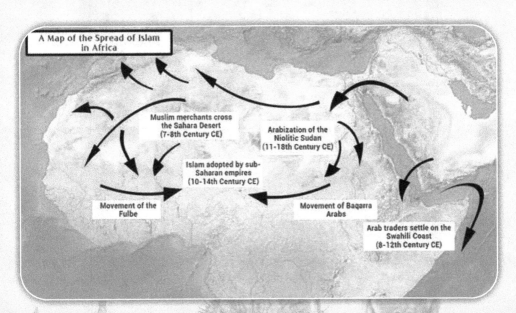

A Map of the Spread of Islam in Africa

Muslim merchants cross the Sahara Desert (7-8th Century CE)

Arabization of the Niolitic Sudan (11-18th Century CE)

Islam adopted by sub-Saharan empires (10-14th Century CE)

Movement of the Fulbe

Movement of Baqarra Arabs

Arab traders settle on the Swahili Coast (8-12th Century CE)

A map indicating the spread of Islam in Africa, 7th to 18th century CE

One of the main reasons Islam spread into Africa was for **trade**. Africa had a rich trade network both within and outside the continent. When the Muslim people came to Africa, they brought their religion with them.

Some kingdoms fully converted to Islam, like the **Mali Empire**. They used Islamic rules to make their laws and built many **mosques**.

COOL FACT: **A mosque is an Islamic place of worship.**

The Great Mosque of Kairouan, 670 CE.
https://commons.wikimedia.org/wiki/File:Great_Mosque_of_Kairouan.jpg#/media/File:Great_Mosque_of_Kairouan.jpg

Other empires, like the **Ghana Empire**, allowed people to convert to Islam, but the rulers never converted. These people allowed Islam and their traditional religions to exist together, so they both influenced each other. African empires converted or **tolerated** Islam because they wanted to continue trading. African leaders believed that adopting this outside religion would strengthen their ties to the merchants. It also helped increase their political power and improved **literacy**.

Fun Fact: The Muslim religious leaders taught people how to read. How do you think people learning how to read could help an empire?

In East Africa, the Islamic people also had to deal with **Christianity**. Christianity had become part of some African countries earlier, like **Nubia**. The Islamic people had to work very hard to convert the people in East Africa to Islam. It was not until the 1300s that many of the African people converted. Can you imagine working to convert someone to an idea or religion for centuries?

The African people got a lot more out of Islam than just a religious system. They also learned a new way to interact with the world.

Fun Fact: Islam is a religion, but it is also a legal and political system. When a country converts to Islam, it can implement laws that closely follow Muslim beliefs.

The people also received better access to trade. Africa was an important part of the trade routes during the Middle Ages, and much wealth came through the Middle East. Trade was a critical part of African culture during this period, and many of the kingdoms grew wealthy. They had important cities where merchants traveled to trade. Africa had a lot to offer the rest of the world!

COOL FACT: Africa traded things like salt and gold. Everyone wanted these things.

The Citadel of Gondershe, Somalia.

Even though Islam was important during the African Middle Ages, the people did not adopt it blindly. Instead, they adapted it to fit their traditions and culture. They blended the two cultures to make something unique. This usually included things like arts. African people already liked geometric designs, and this new religion encouraged it. The people created temples similarly to other Islamic areas, and they made art inspired by their new faith.

Interesting fact: Islam does not allow artists to draw animals or people. Instead, their art has shapes and patterns in it. Can you imagine making art without drawing people or animals?

Just because the African people adopted a new religion didn't mean they gave up their old beliefs. They still worshipped their ancestors and thought their leaders were at least semi-divine. The people made their beliefs their own!

One of the big changes Islam brought to Africa was the creation of a brand-new language. It was called **Kiswahili**. The Muslim people used it to teach people how to read the Koran.

COOL Fact: The Koran is one of the holy books of Islam. Reading the Koran is very important to Muslim people.

The people of Africa were adaptable. They accomplished so much, and their hard work has influenced our modern lives. Let's look at some of the most famous kingdoms in the African Middle Ages to see how the people on this continent thrived!

Can you choose which achievements below came from the African Middle Ages?

- Built the Great Wall of China
- Developed a new language called Kiswahili
- Fought the Vikings
- Built big trading cities and traded gold and salt
- Had famous jousting tournaments
- Housed the Ghana and Mali Empires
- Adapted Islam to their traditions
- Were the first people to discover America

Chapter 2: The Ghana Empire

The Ghana Empire was a powerful kingdom built on trade. They were so important that people crossed the **Sahara Desert** to trade with them.

Fun Fact: The Sahara Desert is the largest warm desert in the world. It is about the size of the United States of America!

The Ghana Empire lasted from about 300 CE to 1200 CE. It was located in Western Africa near the **Niger River**. Today, three different countries control the land the Ghana Empire once ruled: Mali, Mauritania, and Senegal.

Interesting fact: There is a modern African country called Ghana, but it is not related to the Ghana Empire.

Map of the Ghana Empire
Luxo, CC BY-SA 3.0 <http://creativecommons.org/licenses/by-sa/3.0>,
via Wikimedia Commons https://commons.wikimedia.org/wiki/File:Ghana_empire_map.png

Historians think people have lived in West Africa since at least the **Neolithic Period.** Archeologists have found old buildings from the Iron Age, and there was a lot of copper in the area. The metal let the people make tools, and the farmlands let people grow crops. Eventually, the people developed into tribes, and one of them was called the **Soninke people.** They united together under **Dinga Cisse** and started the Ghana Empire.

Historians don't know much about how the Ghana Empire worked in its early days. There aren't a lot of written documents, and archeology can't tell us everything about a culture.

COOL FACT: **The people of Ancient Ghana did not call their kingdom "Ghana." People outside the empire called it that. "Ghana" was a Soninke word that meant "warrior king." The people who lived in the Ghana Empire called it "Wagadou."**

The Ghana Empire had a different political structure than modern Western countries. They did not have a big central government. Instead, they had many villages that were all ruled by a king. The king was an **absolute monarch,** which meant he had all the power and no one could question him. He was in charge of justice and religion. The people treated him with extra care and even made sacrifices in the king's honor. Can you imagine how much the king had to worry about? How would you run a religion if you were in charge?

Most people in Ghana were farmers, but they did not own their land. Instead, each family got a section from the village leader. People grew food like sweet potatoes and grains like rice and millet. The land was good for farming because the Niger River ran through the kingdom. The river also provided fish and birds, so the people usually had plenty to eat.

The king and village leaders lived in the best houses, but most people lived in one-story houses made of mud bricks, wood, and stone. The houses were so effective that people still build houses like this in the area today!

The most important part of the Ghana Empire was the trade routes. They made all their wealth and power because they were on two trade routes. One of those routes ran north to south, and the other ran east to west. The second network of routes was called the **Trans-Saharan Trade Route**.

Fun Fact: The Trans-Saharan Trade Route was at least 600 miles long! People had to cross on foot or in camel caravans.

The people of Ancient Ghana traded with Muslim merchants in big cities. The more they traded, the more powerful they became. Soon, they expanded the empire by taking over smaller kingdoms and tribes around them.

Chinguetti, Ghana Empire.
François COLIN, CC BY-SA 2.5 <https://creativecommons.org/licenses/by-sa/2.5>
via Wikimedia Commons; https://commons.wikimedia.org/wiki/File:Chinguetti-Vue_Goblale_Vielle_ville.jpg

The capital of the Ghana Empire was **Koumbi Saleh**. Historians believe it was a huge city, especially for the medieval era. It took up about 110 acres, and many small villages were around it. A lot of trade took place in the capital. Because many of the traders were Muslim, there was a separate side of the city for them starting in the middle of the 11th century. The Muslim side has twelve mosques! The other side had shrines for the empire's traditional religion. Even though they had different religions, the Ghana Empire and the Islamic traders still worked together.

Koumbi Saleh, Mauritania.

The Ghana Empire traded many different goods, but the most valuable thing they traded was **gold**. The gold mines were south of the early Ghana Empire. For years, the Ghana people traded with the kingdoms south of them to get gold, but as they became more powerful, they expanded their empire and took over the gold mines.

Although gold was the most precious item, the Ghana Empire traded other things. Another important item for trade was **salt**. We might not think salt is very important. It helps food taste good sometimes, but how else does salt affect our daily lives?

For the people in the medieval era, salt was very important. They did not have refrigeration back then, so they used salt to preserve food.

The kingdoms north of Ghana had salt mines. They would mine the salt and then bring it to Ghana to trade. Salt was so important to the people that they sometimes used it as money, just like gold!

The empire also traded goods like ivory, ostrich feathers, and enslaved people. Slavery is not okay, but it was part of the Middle Ages. In return, the empire received copper, horses, and expensive fabrics. Trade networks quickly made Ghana rich!

14

Sadly, the Ghana Empire could not last forever. In the second half of the 11th century, the Islamic people in the north decided to **convert** their neighbors to Islam. When Ghana refused to change its religion to Islam, the Muslim forces attacked them several times. The Muslim forces were called the **Almoravids**. They briefly took over the empire but didn't have enough power to keep it. However, the Ghana Empire never recovered. They had lost a lot of the trade they needed to survive.

Ghana continued to decline into the 12th century. New trade routes opened elsewhere, so people didn't visit the Ghana Empire as much. There was also a bad drought for a few years, and the people struggled to grow food. There was a lot of tension, and civil wars broke out. Can you imagine living in the Ghana Empire during this time? It would have been very hard.

The Ghana Empire continued to crumble until it was absorbed by the Mali Empire. Even though the Ghana Empire is not here today, it was a very important part of medieval Africa. Its people were strong and wealthy because they were good traders.

Chapter 2 Activity

Can you identify which statements are true and which are false?

1. The Ghana Empire was founded by King Soninke.

2. The capital of the Kingdom of Ghana was Koumbi Saleh.

3. The Soninke people were the enemies of the Ghana Empire.

4. After its fall, the Ghana Empire became a part of the Kanem-Bornu Empire.

5. The Ghana Empire made its wealth by trading items like gold and salt.

6. Christians had their own part of the Ghana capital because they traded a lot with the empire.

7. Ghana fell because it was invaded by the Roman Empire.

8. The Ghana Empire was part of the Trans-Saharan Trade Route.

Chapter 3: The Kanem-Bornu Empire

The **Kanem-Bornu Empire** lasted over a thousand years. Its boundaries have changed many times, but it was in a good position on the **Trans-Saharan** Trade Route. The empire stayed in the center of Africa on the eastern shore of **Lake Chad**, even though it went through a lot of change.

COOL FACT: A part of the Kanem-Bornu Empire is still here today! It is called the Borno Emirate, but its people live under the governance of the other countries in the area.

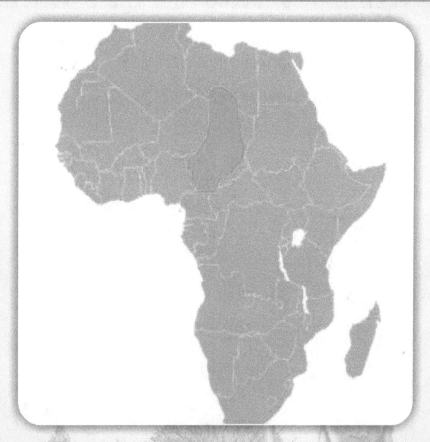

Map of the Kanem-Bornu Empire.
ArnoldPlaton, CC0, via Wikimedia Commons;
https://commons.wikimedia.org/wiki/File:Kanem-Bornu.svg#/media/File:Kanem-Bornu.svg

Before the Kanem-Bornu Empire began, **nomadic** people called the **Zaghawa** and the **Kanembu** were living in the area. Historians think these tribes used to wander in the **Sahara Desert**.

The tribes migrated south and settled on the east side of **Lake Chad**. The Kanembu people started the Kanem Empire around 700 CE. However, it took them a long time to build cities. By the 10th century, it only had two towns, but it was still a very powerful kingdom.

One of the reasons the Kanem Empire became so important is that it was part of the **Trans-Saharan Trade Route**. This empire connected North Africa to Central Africa. It traded many things, like salt, copper, cotton, ostrich feathers, and gold. However, its biggest export was enslaved people, many of whom died trying to get across the Trans-Saharan Trade Route.

The first king of the Kanem Empire was **Sef, or Saif**, and his son was **Dugu**. Dugu started the **Duguwa** dynasty. Instead of calling their rulers kings, the Kanem people called them "**mais.**"

The mais were powerful rulers, and many wanted to expand the Kanem Empire. They had a strong **cavalry**, partly because many people were still nomadic. The cavalry gave their military extra strength.

Expansion and connection to the trade routes brought **Islam** into the Kanem Empire. Around 1085 CE, the Saifawas **deposed** the last king of the Duguwa dynasty. The Saifawas were Muslim and started their own dynasty called the **Sefuwa dynasty**.

Fun Fact: The Sefuwa dynasty made Islam the court and state policy.

The people of the Kanem Empire didn't want to convert to Islam at first. They wanted to keep their old religion. Historians don't know exactly when the Kanem-Bornu Empire became Muslim, but it was popular among the people by the early 1200s.

Fun Fact: In medieval Africa, the people didn't always have the same religion as their king. It was normal for kings to convert to Islam, but the people still practiced their traditional religions. That's one reason the African people were able to adapt Islam to their way of life—there were many other religious influences at the same time!

The Kanem Empire continued to expand. One of its most famous leaders was **Mai Dunama Dabbalemi**, who ruled from 1210 to 1259 CE. He started diplomatic exchanges with the North African sultan; he also created a special hostel in Cairo to help fellow Muslims going to Mecca.

Muslims believe they should take a trip to Mecca at least once in their lives. Mecca is an important holy city for them. These special religious trips are called pilgrimages.

Mai Dunama Dabbalemi is most famous for declaring **jihad** on the tribes around the Kanem Empire.

A jihad is a religious war.

Dabbalemi fought for over seven years and conquered a lot of land. However, he also attacked the **Mune religion**, which made the Tubu and the **Bulala** people angry. The Tubu people didn't fight for long, but the Bulala people fought so much that they accidentally helped start the Bornu Empire.

Flag of Bornu Empire.
https://commons.wikimedia.org/wiki/File:Flag_of_the_Bornu_Empire.svg

Around 1400 CE, there was increasing unrest in Kanem due to civil wars. The Bulala people finally forced the Kanem leader to leave. His name was **Mai Uma b. Idris**. When Mai Idris fled to the west side of Lake Chad, the Kanem rulers became the rulers of **Bornu**, too.

Fun Fact: The people living in Bornu intermarried with the Kanem people. This created a new culture and group of people called the Kanuri.

It took many years for the Kanuri people to settle in Bornu, but once they did, they were stronger than ever. In the early 1500s, they were strong enough to push the Bulala out of Kanem and take back their land.

Group of Kanem-Bu warriors.
https://commons.wikimedia.org/wiki/File:Group_of_Kanem-Bu_warriors.jpg

The Kanem-Bornu Empire was strongest under **Mai Idris Alawma**. He ruled from around 1564 to 1596. Under his rule, the empire was the biggest it would ever be. He made changes to the army to make it better often used a **scorched earth policy** to help his conquests.

Scorched earth policy is when an attacking army burns all the plants in an area. They do this because they don't want the defending army to be able to get food in the wild. It makes people much more dependent on supply lines, which are easier to attack.

Mai Alawma was more than a good military leader who consolidated the empire. He also reformed the government and made the Kanem-Bornu kingdom rich and strong. He even built several new mosques! His hard work made the Kanem-Bornu kingdom strong until the mid-1600s.

The Kanem-Bornu Empire gradually began to fade. They slowly shrank, but it was an important place for Islamic learning in the 17th and 18th centuries. Sadly, even this couldn't save them. The **Fulani** people attacked them in the 1700s, and Kanem-Bornu Empire declined.

The Kanem-Bornu Empire ended around 1900, but it still exists today as Borno Emirate. The Kanuri people were strong and impacted much of African history, leaving a big mark on medieval Africa.

Chapter 3 Activity

Can you put these events in the right order?

1. The reign of King Idris Alawma.

2. The empire was founded by the Zaghawa and Kanembu nomadic people.

3. The Kanem Empire expanded under Mai Dunama Dabbalemi.

4. The Kanuri people recaptured the lost territories and became the Kanem-Bornu Empire.

5. Dugu started the Duguwa dynasty.

6. The Kanem-Bornu Empire ended and became the Borno Emirate.

The **Kingdom of Benin** was a powerful kingdom in West Africa. It was so powerful that European countries like Portugal and Great Britain wanted to trade with it! The Kingdom of Benin was located in the southern part of modern **Nigeria** and ruled from around 1200 CE to 1897 CE.

Fun Fact: The Kingdom of Benin is sometimes called the Kingdom of Edo.

Map of the Kingdom of Benin

The land had a lot of forests, including rainforests, dry forests, and even swamps! According to Benin history, this kingdom began with the **Edo people**. They were tired of their kings, the **Ogisos**, and asked **Prince Oranmiyan** to rule them instead.

Prince Oranmiyan was from the **Kingdom of Ife**. Ife was nearby, but it ruled slightly earlier than the Kingdom of Benin. Ife existed from about 1000 CE to the 1400s CE.

COOL FACT: The Kingdom of Ife was famous for its bronze work. Its people were best at making sculpted heads. Some historians think Ife's culture influenced Benin's as it developed.

Although Prince Oranmiyan was invited to rule the Edo people, the first king of Benin was **Eweka**. Eweka was Prince Oranmiyan's son.

Fun Fact: The Benin people called their king the oba.

Of course, the Kingdom of Benin was not big or powerful when Eweka ruled. He was the first oba! For many years, the political structure was a little complicated. Princes and tribal chiefs ruled some of the land—and some of these chiefs sent tribute to the king.

The **oba** of Benin was a little different from how we might think of a king today. The Benin oba had a divine right to rule.

Interesting fact: The people had many rituals to honor the oba, and one of them was human sacrifice. This was part of their culture until 1897!

The oba was also in charge of all trade with outside powers. Because of Benin's location, it was a good midpoint on trade routes. Benin **facilitated** trade between many African kingdoms, trading things like cotton, yams, salt, and cows.

Around 1450, the **Portuguese** began sailing down the coast of Africa, looking for gold. Although Benin didn't have gold, it did start trading with Portugal. Suddenly, the Kingdom of Benin grew and became very successful because of all this trade. The people traded pepper, ivory, and palm oil with the Europeans.

Sadly, much of Benin's success also came from the **slave trade**. During this time in its history, the Benin kingdom was expanding. The people conquered their neighbors and took the land for their own kingdom. Some tribes willingly sent tribute, including people for slavery, but other tribes were conquered. When Benin attacked a rival tribe, it captured people to sell to Western traders as enslaved people.

Interesting fact: The Western World refers to Europe and America. By the 1600s and 1700s, enslaved people were being moved to the Americas and Europe.

The Kingdom of Benin continued to expand. One of its greatest kings was **Oba Ewuare the Great.** He ruled from 1440 to 1473 CE and was famous as a warrior and magician. Under Ewuare, the role of the oba became **hereditary**.

COOL FACT: A hereditary position is a job or role passed on from parent to child. Usually, sons inherited from their fathers.

Depiction of Benin City.
https://commons.wikimedia.org/wiki/File:Ancient_Benin_City.JPG

Oba Ewuare also expanded the Kingdom of Benin to its largest size. Under his rule, the kingdom became very powerful, and he also rebuilt the capital, **Benin City**.

Drawing of Benin City.
https://commons.wikimedia.org/wiki/File:
Drawing_of_Benin_City_made_by_an_English_officer_1897.jpg

However, the most impressive part of Benin City comes from the royal palace. Many of the pillars in the palace were covered with **brass plaques**. These plaques weren't just pieces of metal, though. They were unique carvings and works of art that told the story of the Benin people.

Single-figure plaque, Benin Kingdom
https://commons.wikimedia.org/wiki/File:Single-figure_plaque,_Benin_Kingdom_court_style,_Edo_peoples,_Benin_City,_Nigeria,_mid_16th_to_17th_century,_cast_copper_alloy_-_Dallas_Museum_of_Art_-_DSC04934.jpg

Many of the brass plaques we still have were most likely made between 1550 and 1650. The artistic pieces have lots of detail, which amazed the Europeans when they first saw them. The Benin people made their art without European influences, proving the people of medieval Africa were full of creativity and innovation.

The plaques show the greatness of the oba. Although they don't tell us anything about commoners or women and children, they show us a lot about how the oba's palace functioned. Because of them, we have a record of many of the obas' achievements through the years. They also show warriors and important battles.

Interesting fact: Many of Benin's brass plaques are now in museums worldwide. You can see them at the British Museum, in Chicago, and even in Berlin!

Benin Kingdom - Warrior and Attendants,
Julia Manzerova, CC BY-SA 2.0 <https://creativecommons.org/licenses/by-sa/2.0>
via Wikimedia Commons, https://commons.wikimedia.org/wiki/File:Benin_kingdom_-_Warrior_and_attendants.jpg

The Kingdom of Benin had beautiful art and left an important impact on West Africa. Sadly, the Kingdom of Benin is not in Africa anymore. In the 1700s and 1800s, Benin began to struggle. The royal family started civil wars for the throne, which weakened the government and economy. Can you imagine trying to keep a strong trade network with wars happening around you? It would be chaos!

There were several weak rulers during this time. They tried to keep Western influences away with their religious rituals, but it wasn't enough to stop the British. The British wanted to control trade in West Africa. When the Kingdom of Benin didn't welcome their merchants, the British invaded. They took Benin City in 1897, burning it. The Kingdom of Benin was officially over.

COOL FACT: Even though the Kingdom of Benin ended in 1897, it eventually became the Republic of Benin in modern Nigeria. Benin City still exists today, and the oba of the city advises the Nigerian government. The oba is no longer king, but he's still important.

The Kingdom of Benin ruled for almost 700 years. In that time, it shaped medieval Africa by creating a strong trade relationship with other kingdoms and the Western World. It also created beautiful art that continues to amaze people today.

Chapter 4 Activity

Can you solve the multiple-choice questions below? Be sure to look over the chapter for the answers!

1. **What is another common name for the Kingdom of Benin?**

    A) Kingdom of Ethiopia   B) Kingdom of Axum   C) Kingdom of Edo

2. **Who first established the Kingdom of Benin?**

    A) Oba Ewuare the Great   B) the Edo people   C) King Solomon

3. **What was the capital of the kingdom?**

    A) Benin City   B) Ife   C) Timbuktu

4. **Who conquered the Kingdom of Benin?**

    A) The French   B) The Egyptians   C) The British

5. **What kind of art is Benin most famous for?**

    A) Paintings   B) Brass plaques   C) Stone sculptures

Chapter 5: The Mali Empire

The **Mali Empire** was huge and wealthy. It ruled much of West Africa from around 1235 CE to 1670 CE. At the height of its power, it had one of the largest armies in the world at that time and was a critical part of the trade networks.

Fun Fact: The Mali Empire is also called the Manding Empire after the people who started it. They were the Mandingo people (also called the Malinke people).

The Mali Empire stretched across many modern countries like Mali, Niger, Guinea, and The Gambia.

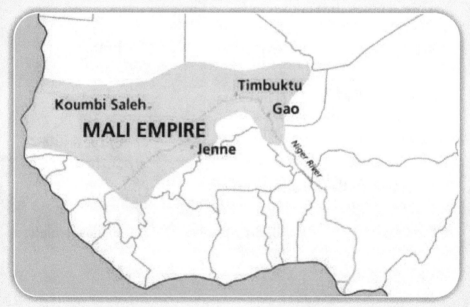

Map of the Mali Empire.
This file is licensed under the Creative Commons Attribution-Share Alike 3.0 Unported license; https://commons.wikimedia.org/wiki/File:MALI_empire_map.PNG

The Malinke people had lived in the area for many years, and they helped the **Ghana Empire** with the gold trade near the end of that empire's reign. As Ghana crumbled at the end of the 1100s, the **Kingdom of Sosso** took over most of the land.

Their ruler was **King Sumanguru**, who started his reign around 1200 CE. He was a bad ruler and was harsh, even imposing trade limits on the Malinke people! The Malinke people were upset about this, so one of their princes named **Sundiata Keita** rose up against the Kingdom of Sosso. He made alliances with other local leaders and defeated the Kingdom of Sosso in 1235 at the Battle of **Krina (or Kirina)**. The Mali Empire had begun, and the land Sundiata Keita won made Mali the largest empire at the time. Throughout the first part of its history, Mali continued to grow to cover about 1,200 miles.

Sundiata also helped set up the Mali Empire's government. The king was an absolute monarch. He had advisors and nobility under his rule, but the king was in charge of running the government and controlling trade.

Trade was very important to the Mali Empire. They were in a perfect place for trade—the Mali Empire even took over areas rich in gold to make its trade even more valuable. Some of these areas were **Galam, Bambuk,** and **Bure.**

However, having gold was only one way the Mali Empire made its vast fortune. It also taxed goods as they came through the empire and sold goods it purchased for higher prices. The Mali Empire also took over **Timbuktu**, an important trade port.

COOL FACT: Timbuktu was started by nomadic people called the Tuaregs around 1100 CE. It was on the Niger River and was a good starting point for the Trans-Saharan Trade Route.

Because of all this trade, the Mali Empire attracted Islamic traders. Of course, Islam had already been in the area, but it eventually became an important part of the empire. The Mansas converted to Islam, but they did not force the commoners to convert. Instead, many people converted on their own. They combined Islam with their traditional **animist** religions to create something unique. As the empire became more powerful, more Islamic scholars and **missionaries** moved to Mali.

Islam became very popular under **Mansa Musa** I. Musa I was one of the most famous kings in medieval Africa. He used his huge army to double the Mali Empire's land.

Djenné Terracotta archer.
https://commons.wikimedia.org/wiki/File:Djenne_Terracotta_Archer_
(13th-15th_cent).jpg#/media/File:Djenne_Terracotta_Archer_(13th-15th_cent).jpg

Fun Fact: Historians think Mansa Musa I's army had about 100,000 soldiers and 10,000 horses. Can you imagine having a group that big?

Djenné Terracotta equestrian.
https://commons.wikimedia.org/wiki/File:
Djenne_Terracotta_Equestrian_(13th-15th_cent).jpg

We'll look into the details of Mansa Musa's life in the next chapter, but when Musa I died around 1332 CE, the Mali Empire was in its **golden age.** He did a lot for Mali. He made the government stronger and brought in a lot of wealth.

COOL FACT: Mansa Musa I was one of the richest people in the history of the world. What would you do if you were one of the richest people today?

He also made a famous **pilgrimage** to **Mecca** in 1324. He gave away so much gold that people were amazed and wanted to visit Mali. When he came back, Musa brought architects, teachers, and poets with him. He wanted Mali to be an important cultural center as well as rich and politically powerful. Musa shaped cities like **Gao** and Timbuktu into major cultural centers. Timbuktu even had a famous school called the **University of Sankore**.

The Djinguereber Mosque, 1327.

Mansa Musa even built mosques! One of those mosques was **Djinguereber**, also known as the Great Mosque of Timbuktu.

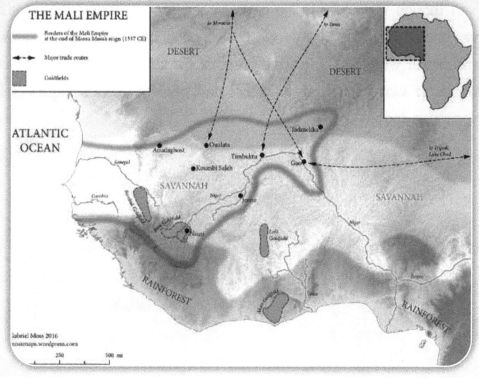

The Mali Empire at the time of Mansa Musa's death.

Gabriel Moss, CC BY-SA 4.0 <https://creativecommons.org/licenses/by-sa/4.0>, via Wikimedia Commons;
https://commons.wikimedia.org/wiki/File:The_Mali_Empire.jpg#/media/File:The_Mali_Empire.jpg

However, the Mali Empire was not able to hold onto its golden age for long. Soon after Musa died, the Mali Empire began losing control of its borderlands. Other groups, like the **Tuareg** and the **Mossi**, attacked, gradually taking over areas. The empire also slipped into civil wars over succession. Because it wasn't clear which relative should be king next, people fought each other for the throne. How do you think that could weaken an empire?

The Mali Empire faded. New trade routes opened up, and these threatened Mali's economy. By 1550, Mali was no longer powerful.

In 1610, Mahmud IV died as the last king. The Mali Empire was over—it was taken into the **Moroccan Empire**.

Even though the Mali Empire is no longer around today, it was still very important. The Mali people built schools and built up impressive amounts of wealth. The empire also made a lasting mark on medieval Africa. It was important to global development, so its legacy still impacts us today.

Chapter 5 Activity

Can you match the king to his achievements? A king might have multiple achievements listed.

Mahmud IV	Sundiata Keita	Mansa Musa I

- United the tribes of the Malinke peoples and formed the Mali Empire

- Developed cities like Timbuktu and Gao into important cultural centers and improved the Mali Empire

- Was the last king of the Mali Empire

- Named the Mali Empire

- Built Djinguereber, the Great Mosque of Timbuktu

Chapter 6: Emperor Mansa Musa

Mansa Musa I was one of the most famous African rulers from the medieval era. He came to the throne of the **Mali Empire** around 1312 CE. He led the Mali Empire through its golden age and was famous for his great wealth. Under his rule, the Mali Empire became a great place of learning and creativity.

Fun Fact: Musa is the Arabic form of the name Moses. Moses was an important Israelite leader, and Jews, Christians, and Muslims still honor him today.

Ruler Mansa Musa.

The king before Mansa Musa was **Muhammad ibn Qu**. Some stories say Muhammad wanted to explore the Atlantic Ocean and set out on a voyage. Muhammad made Musa the ruler until he returned, but then he never came back. Thus, Musa became the next Mansa.

Interesting fact: Not all historians agree with this story. Some think Mansa made up this story after getting rid of Muhammad, but no one knows for sure.

Mansa Musa I was young when he became the leader of the Mali Empire. Historians think he was in his early twenties. Can you imagine running a huge empire as a young adult?

He spent most of his early reign expanding the empire. His army was huge! It had about 100,000 soldiers and 10,000 horses. With his huge army, Musa doubled the Mali Empire.

COOL FACT: **The Mali Empire was the second-largest empire in the world at the time. It was only smaller than the Mongol Empire.**

He knew he needed help governing all of this land, so he set up provinces ruled by governors. His administration did more recordkeeping that was all sent to **Niani**, the capital, and worked hard to improve the cities. Musa made the empire even more wealthy by increasing taxes, making conquered tribes pay tribute, and using Mali's gold and copper mines.

While Mansa Musa I was conquering the tribes and cities around him, he also captured people. Many of these people became enslaved. Slavery was another way the Mali Empire gained wealth, but it was still wrong.

Seventeen years into his reign, Musa I decided to take a **pilgrimage** to **Mecca**. He left the Mali Empire in 1324 with an impressive **entourage**. An entourage is a group of people who help a specific person, usually someone famous or important. Musa's entourage had about 60,000 people!

Fun Fact: **Musa brought a lot of gold with him. He also paid for everything the people and animals on the trip needed. Can you imagine how much that cost?**

Travel during the Middle Ages was different than travel today. People could not drive down highways or take flights. Instead, people had to walk or ride animals everywhere. Musa rode a horse and brought at least eighty camels with him on his trip to Mecca.

Fun Fact: His trip to Mecca and back was at least 4,000 miles. How long do you think it would take to walk that far?

Mansa Musa on his way to Mecca, c. 1670.
https://commons.wikimedia.org/wiki/File:Mansa-Musa-on-his-way-to-Mecca-Credit-Print-Collector-Getty-images-1536x790.jpg

Musa made a huge impact when he arrived in **Cairo**, Egypt, in July 1324. He was generous and polite, but his journey was about more than just going to Mecca. He was also showing off his empire's wealth, which intrigued people across the Middle East and Europe. It made people want to visit the Mali Empire.

Mansa Musa I stayed in Cairo for three months. He met with the Cairo leader named **al-Nasir Muhammad**. Their first meeting was tense. Al-Nasir wanted Musa to pay **homage**.

COOL FACT: Homage is a special way of giving honor or respect to somebody. Al-Nasir wanted Musa to bow down before him. Musa finally agreed if he was really bowing to Allah, the Arabian name for God.

Thankfully, the two rulers became more friendly after that. Musa had a palace while he stayed in Cairo, and his entourage spent lots of gold in the marketplaces. They spent and gave away so much gold that they actually decreased its value for about twelve years.

In October 1324, Musa continued his journey to Mecca, where he bought land to help future people from Mali make pilgrimages. He was impressed with the holy buildings in Mecca and decided he wanted similar buildings in Mali.

COOL FACT: While Musa was making his pilgrimage, his general, Sagmandia, conquered the city of Gao for Mali. When Musa returned, both Gao and Timbuktu submitted to his authority.

Musa brought back architects and scholars to make the Mali Empire even better. He ordered several mosques to be built in Gao and Timbuktu. The most famous mosque was the **Great Mosque** in Timbuktu. It is also called the **Djinguereber**. The building was completed around 1330 and made from beaten earth supported by wood. The wood usually sticks out of the building, which makes Mali's architecture unique.

Musa did more than just construct beautiful buildings, though. He also wanted people to be avid learners, so he created schools and universities. In Timbuktu, the **University of Sankore** became a center of learning for things like religion, math, and astronomy. The city soon became famous for trade, learning, and Islamic activities, and people hurried to visit.

Education and more religious devotion were big parts of Mansa Musa's reign. He led the Mali Empire through the best time in its history, making it large and powerful. However, one of Mansa Musa I's biggest impacts on world history was his pilgrimage. He showed off Mali's wealth so effectively that people soon spread the word about it. The stories even reached Europe. In 1375, a Spanish mapmaker created the *Catalan Atlas*. It is a map of West Africa, and it shows Musa sitting on his throne with gold all around him.

Musa depicted holding an imperial golden globe, 1375.
https://commons.wikimedia.org/wiki/File:Catalan_Atlas_BNF_Sheet_6_Mansa_Musa_(cropped).jpg

The Europeans were fascinated by the legendary amounts of gold in Mali. Their curiosity eventually led to explorations. They sailed across the seas, looking for new trade routes and lands. Mansa Musa's pilgrimage ended up changing the world forever.

Interesting fact: Historians don't know exactly when Musa died. Some historians think he died in 1332 CE, but some think he died in 1337 CE.

The Mali Empire lasted long after Mansa Musa died, but it would never be the same. His work changed the empire and the world, inspiring people to search for wealth and to hold to their religious ideas.

Can you put these events in timeline order?

1. The pilgrimage to Mecca.

2. Mansa Musa started his reign.

3. The Catalan Atlas was made with Musa on it.

4. He revitalized and improved cities.

5. He built the Great Mosque at Timbuktu.

6. Sagmandia conquered Gao.

Chapter 7: The Kingdom of Abyssinia

The **Kingdom of Abyssinia** ruled from about 1270 CE to 1974 in modern-day **Ethiopia**. This country is in East Africa, and it has a very long history. In fact, Ethiopia is one of the oldest countries in the world!

Fun Fact: The Kingdom of Abyssinia is also called the Kingdom of Ethiopia.

Map of Abyssinia

https://commons.wikimedia.org/wiki/File:1818_Pinkerton_Map_of_Nubia,_
Sudan_and_Abyssinia_-_Geographicus_-_Abyssinia-pinkerton-1818.jpg

Two kingdoms ruled the area before the Kingdom of Abyssinia. The first was the **Kingdom of Axum**. They ruled from the 1st century CE until the 8th century CE. Axum was the first sub-Saharan country to adopt Christianity, and they were so dedicated to it that people have practiced Christianity there ever since.

The Kingdom of Abyssinia was one of the few predominately Christian kingdoms in medieval Africa.

After Axum faded, the **Zagwe dynasty** took over the area. It ruled the area until 1270 CE and expanded Ethiopian lands. Zagwe was also a Christian kingdom, and churches were important to the people.

Ethiopia was safe from Muslim armies for a long time because it had been hospitable during Muhammad's lifetime. The Ethiopian people were allowed to practice Christianity without pressure to convert to Islam like many countries around them.

The most famous king of Zagwe was **Gebre Mesqel Lalibela**. He carved churches out of rock, which impressed the people. One of the most famous is the Church of Saint George at Lalibela. It was carved in the shape of a cross.

Church of Saint George at Lalibela, Ethiopia, 11-12th century CE.
Jialiang Gao www.peace-on-earth.org, CC BY-SA 3.0 <http://creativecommons.org/licenses/by-sa/3.0/>, via Wikimedia Commons; https://commons.wikimedia.org/wiki/File:Bete_Giyorgis_Lalibela_Ethiopia.jpg#/media/lang=de#file

In 1270, the **Solomonid dynasty** ended the Zagwe dynasty and started the Kingdom of Abyssinia. The Solomonid dynasty claimed they were descended from King Solomon and the Queen of Sheba.

Interesting fact: King Solomon was an Israelite king recorded in the Old Testament of the Bible. The Queen of Sheba came to visit him. The Solomonid dynasty believes the two had a child named Menelik, who started the dynasty.

In 1270 CE, the dynasty was led by **Yekuno Amlak**. He overthrew the last Zagwe king and started his own kingdom.

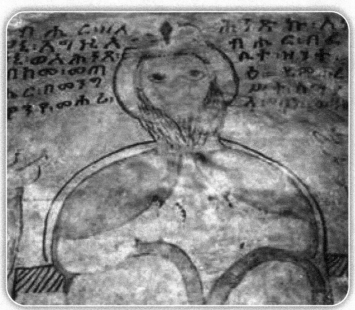

Contemporary portrait of Yekuno Amlak,
founder of the Ethiopian Empire.

Like many other countries, the Kingdom of Abyssinia wanted to expand its lands and have more trading opportunities. The Abyssinians fought with Muslims in the area over who owned the coastlands—an important part of the trade routes. However, Abyssinia had better success with trade on the Blue Nile and over land.

Abyssinia used several techniques to get more land: religion, warfare, and diplomacy. It tended to target areas that were not Christian.

Most of the people around the Kingdom of Abyssinia were Muslim or still followed traditional African religions. There weren't a lot of other Christian countries in Africa at this time.

Abyssinian King Yagbea-Sion and his forces.
https://commons.wikimedia.org/wiki/File:YagbeaSionBattlingAdaSultan.JPG

The king encouraged people to move into newly-conquered territory by offering them pieces of land. This was called a **gult**. People who accepted land from the king could make the farmers on the land pay tribute, so it was a popular way for Abyssinia to maintain its hold on new lands.

One of the most famous Abyssinian rulers was **Amda Seyon I**. He ruled from 1314 to 1344 CE, and he is most famous for expanding Abyssinia.

Fasilides Palace.
Bernard Gagnon, CC BY-SA 3.0 <https://creativecommons.org/licenses/by-sa/3.0>,
via Wikimedia Commons; https://commons.wikimedia.org/wiki/File:Fasilides_Palace_02.jpg

Even though the Kingdom of Abyssinia wanted to expand its lands, many of its wars also focused on spreading Christianity. These were also **holy wars**. When **Zera Yakob** reigned in the 15th century, he defeated the Muslim countries on the coastlands.

Because Christianity was an important part of the kingdom, Abyssinia was also connected to Europe. During the Crusades, European countries tried to convince the Abyssinians to join them, but they did not help the Europeans in those holy wars.

Interesting fact: The Crusades were a series of wars the Europeans fought with the Muslims over the Holy Land. The Holy Land is in modern-day Israel and is an important place for Judaism, Christianity, and Islam.

Sadly, because it fought the Muslims throughout much of its history, the Kingdom of Abyssinia was no longer safe from the Muslim armies. The Muslim states banded together in the 1500s and attacked Abyssinia. They destroyed churches and even sacked **Axum**, one of the kingdom's major cities. The Kingdom of Abyssinia continued to weaken, but it had a revival in the mid-1800s.

COOL FACT: Ethiopia is one of two African countries that did not fall to colonialism. Colonialism is when a powerful country takes over a less powerful nation to take their resources. The Italians tried to take over Ethiopian land in 1896, but the Ethiopians pushed them back. They were able to keep their freedom and their country.

The Kingdom of Abyssinia finally ended in 1974 CE. Their last king was **Haile Selassie**. He wanted the government to become a **constitutional monarchy**, which would have given him a lot of power. However, the common people didn't think they had a voice in the government. When Haile Selassie did not try to help the people during famines in 1972 and 1974, they revolted and turned to **Marxist** ideas. In 1974, the Kingdom of Abyssinia fell, and **communism** took over the country.

The Kingdom of Abyssinia was an old kingdom. It saw many changes during its time in Africa and greatly impacted African culture. It reminds us that Africa developed many powerful civilizations during its history. Abyssinia had strong armies and a strong hold on its religion, impacting African history to this day.

Chapter 7 Activity

Can you answer the following questions in one to two sentences?

1. Who established the Kingdom of Abyssinia?

2. When was the kingdom established?

3. What other name is sometimes used to describe the Kingdom of Abyssinia?

4. Who was Yekuno Amlak?

5. What three techniques did the Kingdom of Abyssinia use to conquer land?

6. How long did the Kingdom of Abyssinia last?

Chapter 8: The Songhay Kingdom

The **Songhay Kingdom** was the last major pre-colonial kingdom in West Africa. At the height of its power, it stretched from the Atlantic Ocean to modern Niger. It ruled in West Africa from about 1464 to 1591 CE.

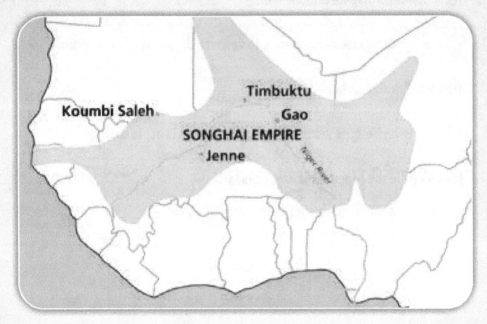

Songhay Empire map
No machine-readable author provided. Roke~commonswiki assumed (based on copyright claims).,
CC BY-SA 3.0 <http://creativecommons.org/licenses/by-sa/3.0/>,
via Wikimedia Commons https://commons.wikimedia.org/wiki/File:SONGHAI_empire_map.PNG

The Songhay people had actually been in the area since about 800 CE. They founded **Gao** as their capital, but it eventually became part of the Mali Empire. As the Mali Empire began to fade in the 1460s, the Songhay people rose up once again.

Fun Fact: The Songhay Kingdom never completely defeated the Mali Empire, but it soon became more powerful than Mali. The Mali Empire continued on the western edge of Songhay land until the 1600s.

Even though it had been part of the Mali Empire for many years, Songhay never really submitted to Mali's rule. The Songhay people controlled transportation on the Niger River, which made them powerful. In the 1400s, they began **raiding** Mali cities. Because of their constant fighting, the Songhay people finally won their freedom.

King Sunni Ali was the first Songhay ruler. He conquered cities like Timbuktu and gave his kingdom a strong start.

After King Sunni Ali died in 1492, his son took the throne, but he lost it after only one year to **Askia Muhammad Touré (Muhammed I).**

Interesting fact: Muhammad had to overthrow Sunni Ali's son to take the throne. **His name was Sunni Baru.**

Even though Muhammad I was a usurper, he still led the Songhay Kingdom during its golden age.

Fun Fact: "Askia" means "ruler" or "emperor."

Askia Muhammad I ruled from 1494 to 1528 CE. He expanded the empire even more, making the kingdom the largest it would ever be, and set up **provinces**. He set up the kingdom's first professional army and marched southeast, conquering land between the Niger River and Lake Chad.

Of course, Askia Muhammad was more than just a conqueror. He also invested in his kingdom. He made the government stronger by centralizing it.

COOL FACT: The king of Songhay was an absolute monarch, but there were many ministers and officials to help the king run the kingdom.

Muhammad was a Muslim, so he enforced Islamic laws and sent ambassadors to other Muslim states. He also built many schools throughout the kingdom and expanded Timbuktu's **University of Sankore.**

One of the main areas Askia Muhammad wanted the Songhay Kingdom to grow was trade. The Mali Empire had grown wealthy from trade because it had gold mines on its southern borders, but the Songhay Kingdom didn't have these.

In 1471, the **Portuguese** had sailed to West Africa and set up their own trading post. This trading post was another option that challenged the Trans-Saharan Trade Route. The Songhay Kingdom had to work hard to keep its resources and benefit from trade. They **monopolized** the Trans-Saharan Trade Route.

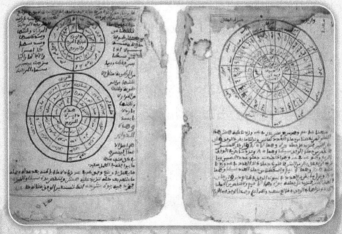

The Timbuktu Manuscripts.
https://commons.wikimedia.org/wiki/File:Timbuktu-manuscripts-astronomy-mathematics.jpg

To monopolize something means someone has full control over creating or giving an item or service. How might a monopoly on the Trans-Saharan Trade Route have helped the Songhay Kingdom?

Timbuktu remained a thriving trade center. The Songhay Kingdom traded things like gold, spices, kola nuts, and enslaved people in exchange for salt, sugar, glass, and horses. Trade centers were not just markets. Instead, they were cities with schools, mosques, and houses built with stone. Most commoners lived on the city's outskirts in mud or reed houses, and farming remained an important part of their lives.

The Tomb of Askia in Gao.
Taguelmoust, CC BY-SA 3.0 <http://creativecommons.org/licenses/by-sa/3.0>
via Wikimedia Commons, https://commons.wikimedia.org/wiki/File:Askia.jpg

When Askia Muhammad I died in 1528, he left behind a strong kingdom. It flourished for many years, and trade continued to support major cities like Timbuktu, Gao, and Djenné. Sadly, the Songhay Kingdom also had many civil wars after Muhammad died. People fought over the throne, and all of the wars weakened the kingdom. When another civil war erupted in 1591, **Sultan Ahmad I al-Mansur, a Saadi sultan,** decided to attack.

COOL FACT: Sultan Ahmad I al-Mansur was the leader of Morocco. He wanted to control West Africa because he wanted the gold mines.

Askia Ishaq II was the last Songhay king, and he had an army with 30,000 soldiers and 10,000 cavalry riders. Ahmad I only sent 4,000 Moroccan soldiers to defeat the Songhay Kingdom, but they had new technology—muskets and cannons. The Songhay people were still fighting with arrows and spears, so the Moroccan army had the better weapons.

The Moroccans defeated the Songhay Kingdom and made it part of the Moroccan Empire. However, the Songhay people did not accept defeat quietly. They gave the Moroccans the same trouble they had given the Mali Empire. They rebelled and fought back, but it wasn't enough to save their kingdom. The Songhay Kingdom faded as the last of the powerful West African kingdoms.

The Songhay people were strong and determined to rule their own lives. They understood the importance of trade and believed in education and advancements. Although it no longer exists, the Songhay Kingdom shows how powerful the medieval African kingdoms were and the impact they made on the world.

Chapter 8 Activity

Can you decide which questions are true and which are false?

1. The Songhay Kingdom was founded by Emperor Mansa.

2. The Mali Empire ruled the Songhay Empire before Sunni Ali liberated it.

3. The empire reached its peak under the reign of Askia Muhammad.

4. The Moroccans invaded and conquered Gao and Timbuktu.

5. Askia Muhammad was a Christian and enforced Christianity during his reign.

6. The Moroccans beat the Songhay Kingdom because they had muskets and cannons.

7. The Songhay people were new to the area in 1461.

Chapter 9: Society and Famous Rulers

Medieval Africa had many famous rulers. They impacted their kingdoms' religion and daily lives and had a big impact on the world! Let's look at some of the most famous rulers from medieval Africa.

King Idris Alawma

King Idris Alawma was one of the greatest rulers of the **Kanem-Bornu Empire**. His reign started around 1564CE, but when he started his rule, Kanem and Bornu were separated. Bornu was ruling the empire by itself.

King Alawma wanted to expand his territory, so he made some changes to his military. He gave them new equipment like firearms, chainmail, and iron helmets. Idris Alawma also added musketeers, organized a new advanced guard and rear guard, and often used scorched earth policy to help his conquests. Alawma was an excellent military leader and reconquered Kanem. This re-solidified the Kanem-Bornu Empire.

However, political conquest was not his only focus. He also wanted to improve the government to better help the empire. He separated the **judiciary** branch from the rest of the government.

COOL FACT: The judiciary branch handles court cases and makes judgments when people break the law. What countries today separate their courts from other parts of the government?

Alawma also practiced Islam and encouraged his people to adopt the religion. He built new mosques and wanted people to make pilgrimages to Mecca. He worked hard with the Ottoman Empire to keep his people safe on their travels. The Kanem-Bornu Empire became more connected to the Muslim countries around them and did well under his rule.

Oba Ewuare the Great

Oba Ewuare the Great was one of the most famous rulers of the **Benin Empire**. He ruled from 1440 to 1473 CE and was remembered as a wise man. The oral stories say he was a great magician and warrior. While Ewuare led Benin, he added many new areas, including 201 new towns. He was certainly a good military leader!

Ewuare also focused on making the capital better. The capital city, called **Benin City**, received new roads and gateways while he ruled. Benin City was impressively organized. Oba Ewuare gave the city huge walls and a moat. The city was divided into districts. People grouped together in each district to practice their crafts and trades.

Oba Ewuare the Great.

During his reign, Ewuare also encountered the **Portuguese**, sailing down the West African coast looking for new trade opportunities. Ewuare helped them build trade with the Benin Empire. This helped the empire grow economically. Under his rule, the empire prospered. Ewuare even encouraged people to make art, like wood and ivory carvings. Oba Ewuare the Great was one of the greatest Benin leaders and helped make the empire powerful.

Amda Seyon I

Amda Seyon I was one of the great leaders of the **Kingdom of Abyssinia**. He took the throne around 1314 CE and ruled until 1344 CE. He is most famous for doubling the size of the kingdom. Under his rule, Abyssinia reached from the Rift Valley to the Red Sea. Amda Seyon I also secured control over the central and southern parts of his kingdom, which had been less secure before.

COOL FACT: Amda Seyon I also dealt with succession issues by putting all of his male relations in a monastery except his sons. It kept the men from fighting civil wars for the throne. How would you feel about having to live in a monastery because you were related to the king?

Amda Seyon did not tolerate rebellions, and he treated the Muslim countries around him harshly. When lands under his power tried to break away, he killed anyone involved. Even though he was very harsh, Amda Seyon I created a strong kingdom that ruled the area for hundreds of years. He also encouraged trade. Historians believe the Kingdom of Abyssinia traded with the Byzantine Empire. They didn't only trade resources—they also exchanged books and written documents. Under Amda Seyon, Abyssinia's influence grew and changed the world.

An Ethiopian depiction of Amda Seyon I.

Dawit II

Dawit II was a king of **Abyssinia** who ruled from around 1508 to 1540. His reign was very different than the rule of Amda Seyon. The Muslim forces had grown strong in the years since then, and they attacked starting in the 1520s. Dawit spent most of his reign fighting against them, but the Muslim armies gained ground.

Although Dawit II was not the last leader of Abyssinia, his rule was a dark time. There was a lot of fighting, and the Christian forces were struggling. He finally reached out to **Portugal** to ask for help, but they did not arrive until after he died in 1540. Thankfully, Abyssinia did not fall, but they were much smaller now. The kingdom would never be the same again.

Sunni Ali

Sunni Ali was the first king of the **Songhay Kingdom**—he began his rule around 1464. The Songhay Kingdom had just freed itself from the Mali Empire, which was falling apart. Sadly, they did not get a lot of land out of it. All they had was **Gao**, their capital.

COOL FACT: Gao was a strong trading center, but the Songhay Kingdom needed more than one city if they were going to survive.

Around 1468, Sunni Ali decided to put his military skills to use. He attacked cities like Mema, Djenné, and Timbuktu and captured them. He made sure his kingdom was connected to the Trans-Saharan Trade Route and defeated other tribes that would have attacked Songhay. This added new trading opportunities for the Songhay Kingdom, and the new lands brought wealth into the kingdom.

Sunni Ali was a talented military commander, but he was not always kind to the people he conquered. He was also known as **Sunni the Merciless**.

COOL FACT: Ali's army had a special advantage over the cities it attacked. It had an armored cavalry and the only navy in North Africa."

Although some of his methods were cruel, he is remembered today for giving his kingdom the foundation it needed to be strong for many years.

Askia Muhammad

Askia Muhammad ruled the **Songhay Kingdom** from 1494 to 1528 CE. He was a general under King Sunni Ali, but after he died around 1492, Muhammad decided to take the throne for himself.

Interesting fact: Muhammad had to overthrow Sunni Ali's son to take the throne. His name was Sunni Baru.

Muhammad was a good general but was even better at organizing a government. The new kingdom needed structure. He split the kingdom into **provinces** and set up a standing army. However, Muhammad was also a Muslim, so part of organizing the Songhay Kingdom included adding **Islamic laws**.

COOL FACT: Many of the Islamic laws are found in the Koran.

The Songhay Kingdom made **Arabic** its official written language, but it also made Islam the official religion for the nobility. Instead of encouraging people to adopt it, this made people leery of it. Still, the Songhay Kingdom became influential under Askia Muhammad, changing kingdoms beyond their borders.

Chapter 9 Activity

Can you match the rulers to their kingdoms? There might be more than one ruler per kingdom.

King Idris Alawma

Askia Muhammad

Oba Ewuare the Great

Amda Seyon I

Sunni Ali

Dawit II

Mansa Musa

The Songhay Kingdom

The Kingdom of Abyssinia

The Kingdom of Benin

The Kanem—Bornu Empire

Mali Empire

Chapter 10: Culture and Art

Medieval Africa was filled with many different kingdoms. They had great armies and were essential to global trade. Although they were powerful and changed the world, these kingdoms also produced beautiful art.

Some of this art came from the buildings they constructed. The Mali Empire built several mosques, and one of the most famous is the **Great Mosque of Djenné.**

Fun Fact: Djenné was an important city in the Mali Empire. It was part of the Trans-Saharan Trade Route and is one of the oldest cities in sub-Saharan Africa.

The Great Mosque at Djenné was built in the 1200s, but it was expanded multiple times. Because Mali could not access many stones, it was made from mud bricks and plaster. The building is a big rectangle, and it has a courtyard and a **prayer hall.** The prayer hall is so big that 3,000 people can fit inside! The mosque was built with traditional Mali architecture, with wooden beams sticking out of the walls to support the mud and plaster.

The Great Mosque of Djenné.

Buildings made of mud need more plaster every year to keep them in good shape. Can you imagine having to redo the walls of the Great Mosque in Djenné every year?

The Mali Empire also built the **Great Mosque of Timbuktu**. Timbuktu had many important buildings, especially when it became an important place for Muslim education. The Great Mosque in Timbuktu is one of three important mosques in the city.

Mansa Musa built the Great Mosque between 1325 and 1327, right after he returned from his pilgrimage to Mecca. This building has some, but most of it is built similarly to the Great Mosque in Djenné. The mud and wood buildings were traditional in Mali, but they required a lot of work to maintain!

Not all of the buildings constructed in Medieval Africa were mosques. In the Kingdom of Abyssinia, one of the most famous buildings is the **Church of Saint George** at Lalibela.

Lalibela was an Ethiopian ruler, and he was so influential they renamed the city after him. One of his favorite activities was building churches.

According to legend, Lalibela had a vision. He was visited by an angel who told him how to build a church that would bring Heaven to Earth. Historians don't know if he really had a vision, but Lalibela immediately started building the Church of Saint George after that.

The church is special because it is carved out of volcanic rock. It's shaped like a cross and has many windows. The walls of the church stand over thirty yards high. That is over ninety feet tall! People had to carve tunnels to get to the church and then carve out the inside.

The inside of the church is beautiful. It is covered in **frescoes** about St. George and King Lalibela.

Church of Saint George.

These buildings show how beautiful architecture was during the Middle Ages in Africa. The people were imaginative and talented, but they didn't stop at buildings. They also made smaller pieces of art, like sculptures and pottery, and every empire had its own style. As you might remember, the Kingdom of Benin had special **brass plaques** in the palace filled with details about the king's life. They showed important leaders and warriors and decorated the pillars. Carving these scenes into the brass would have been difficult, but they did it without outside help.

Of course, there were other kinds of art. Art also includes written documents. One of the most famous written texts from Medieval Africa comes from the Mali Empire, and it is called the **Timbuktu Manuscripts**.

Because Timbuktu was an academic center for hundreds of years, many people traveled from all over the world to learn. They didn't just learn about Islam. They also learned about biology, astronomy, math, and even music. Experts wrote down many things they were learning by hand and carefully saved them.

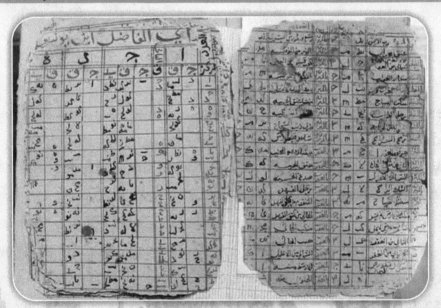

A manuscript page from Timbuktu showing a table of astronomical information.
https://commons.wikimedia.org/wiki/File:Timbuktu-manuscripts-astronomy-tables.jpg
#/media/File:Timbuktu-manuscripts-astronomy-tables.jpg

There are over 40,000 pages in the Timbuktu Manuscripts, some of which were written in the 11th century. That was about a thousand years ago! Although some of the writing talks about **secular** topics, it also has early Qurans. It is an important national treasure for Mali, even though the empire has faded. The manuscripts remind the world that medieval Africa was a time filled with new discoveries as people explored the world around them and taught others about it.

Manuscript of Nasir al-Din Abu.

Medieval Africa was a vibrant time in African history. Many of the kingdoms and empires were heavily involved in trade. They changed the way people thought about travel and wealth. The people of Africa also adopted Islam into their culture, but they didn't get rid of their old beliefs and traditions. Instead, they merged new ideas with old ideas, creating something unique. Their leaders were strong warriors and government organizers, and their art reminds us that beauty is everywhere. We still have much to learn from medieval Africa, but it was an important part of how the world developed into what we know today.

Chapter 10 Activity

Can you pick which of the following monuments are from medieval Africa?

- St. Peter's Basilica

- Djinguereber Mosque

- Hagia Sophia

- Great Mosque of Djenné

- The Eiffel Tower

- Westminster Abbey

- Church of Saint George

Answer Key

Chapter : 1

Can you choose which of the achievements below came from the African Middle Ages?

- ~~Built the Great Wall of China~~
- Developed a new language called Kiswahili
- ~~Fought the Vikings~~
- Built big trading cities and traded gold and salt
- ~~Had famous jousting tournaments~~
- Housed the Ghana and Mali Empires
- Adapted Islam to their traditions
- ~~Were the first people to discover America.~~

Chapter : 2

1. The Ghana Empire was founded by King Soninke.False
2. The capital of the Kingdom of Ghana was Koumbi Saleh.True
3. The Soninke people were the enemies of the Ghana Empire. False
4. After its fall, the Ghana Empire became a part of the Kanem-Bornu Empire.False
5. The Ghana Empire made its wealth by trading items like gold and salt.True
6. Christians had their own part of the Ghana capital because they traded a lot with the empire.False
7. Ghana fell because they were invaded by the Roman Empire.False
8. The Ghana Empire was part of the Trans-Saharan Trade Route.True

Chapter : 3

2. The empire was founded by the Zaghawa and Kanembu nomadic people.

5. Dugu started the Duguwa dynasty.

3. The Kanem Empire expanded under Mai Dunama Dabbalemi.

4. Bornu recaptured its lost territories and became the Kanem-Bornu Empire.

1. The reign of King Idris Alawma.

6. The Kanem-Bornu Empire ended and became the Borno Emirate.

Chapter : 4

1. What is another common name for the Kingdom of Benin?

    A) Kingdom of Ethiopia   B) Kingdom of Axum **C) the Kingdom of Edo**

2. Who first established the Kingdom of Benin?

    A) Oba Ewuare the Great **B) the Edo people**   C) King Solomon

3. What was the capital of the kingdom?

    A) Benin City   B) Ife   C) Timbuktu

4. Who conquered the Kingdom of Benin?

    A) The French   B) The Egyptians   **C) The British**

5. What kind of art is Benin most famous for?

    A) Paintings   **B) Brass plaques**   C) Stone sculptures

Chapter : 5

Can you match the king to his achievements? A king might have multiple achievements listed.

Mahmud IV   Sundiata Keita   Mansa Musa I

- United the tribes of the Malinke peoples and formed the Mali EmpireSundiata Keita

- Developed cities like Timbuktu and Gao into important cultural centers and improved the Mali EmpireMansa Musa I

- Was the last king of the Mali EmpireMahmud IV

- Name the Mali EmpireSundiata Keita

- Built Djinguereber, Timbuktu's Great MosqueMansa Musa I

Chapter : 6

2. Mansa Musa started his reign.

4. He revitalized and improved cities.

1. The pilgrimage to Mecca.

6. Sagmandia conquered Gao.

5. He built the Great Mosque at Timbuktu.

3. The *Catalan Atlas* was made with Musa on it.

Chapter : 7

1. Who established the Kingdom of Abyssinia?

   Yekuno Amlak started the Kingdom of Abyssinia.

2. When was the kingdom established?

   It was established in 1270 CE.

3. What other name is sometimes used to describe the Kingdom of Abyssinia?

   The Kingdom of Abyssinia is also called the Kingdom of Ethiopia.

4. Who was Yekuno Amlak?

   He was the first king of Abyssinia. He came from the Solomonid dynasty.

5. What three techniques did the Kingdom of Abyssinia use to conquer land?

   They used religion, warfare, and diplomacy.

6. How long did the Kingdom of Abyssinia last?

   The Kingdom of Abyssinia ended in 1974.

Chapter : 8

1. The Songhay Kingdom was founded by Emperor Mansa.**False**

2. The Songhay Kingdom was ruled by the Mali Empire before Sunni Ali liberated it.**True**

3. The empire reached its peak under the reign of Askia Muhammad.**True**

4. The Moroccans invaded and conquered Gao and Timbuktu.**True**

5. Askia Muhammad was a Christian and enforced Christianity during his reign.**False**

6. The Moroccans beat the Songhay Kingdom because they had muskets and cannons. **True**

7. The Songhay people were new to the area in 1461.**False**

Chapter : 9

King Idris Alawma— The Kanem–Bornu Empire

Askia Muhammad— Songhay Kingdom

Oba Ewuare the Great— The Kingdom of Benin

Amda Seyon I— The Kingdom of Abyssinia

Sunni Ali— Songhay Kingdom

Dawit II— The Kingdom of Abyssinia

Mansa Musa— Mali Empire

Chapter : 10

- ~~St. Peter's Basilica~~
- Djinguereber Mosque
- ~~Hagia Sophia~~
- Great Mosque of Djenné
- ~~The Eiffel Tower~~
- ~~Westminster Abbey~~
- Church of Saint George

If you want to learn more about tons of other exciting historical periods, check out our other books!

ANCIENT AFRICA FOR KIDS

A CAPTIVATING GUIDE TO ANCIENT AFRICAN CIVILIZATIONS, EMPIRES, AND HISTORY

CAPTIVATING HISTORY

Bibliography

"Ancient Africa for Kids: Empire of Ancient Ghana." Ducksters. Technological Solutions, Inc. (TSI). Accessed April 2023. https://www.ducksters.com/history/africa/empire_of_ancient_ghana.php.

"Ancient Africa for Kids: Empire of Ancient Mali." Ducksters. Technological Solutions, Inc. (TSI). Accessed April 2023. https://www.ducksters.com/history/africa/empire_of_ancient_mali.php.

"Amda Seyon." *EthiopianHistory*.com. Accessed April 2023. https://ethiopianhistory.com/Amda_Seyon/.

"Amda Seyon I Facts for Kids." *Kiddle Encyclopedia.* February 2023. https://kids.kiddle.co/Amda_Seyon_I.

"Bornu Empire." *Lumen Learning*. Accessed April 2023. https://courses.lumenlearning.com/suny-hccc-worldcivilization/chapter/bornu-empire/.

Britannica, T. Editors of Encyclopedia. "Benin." *Encyclopedia Britannica*. March 2023. https://www.britannica.com/place/Benin-historical-kingdom-West-Africa.

---. "Ghana." *Encyclopedia Britannica*. March 2023. https://www.britannica.com/place/Ghana-historical-West-African-empire.

---. "Kanem-Bornu." *Encyclopedia Britannica*. April 2023. https://www.britannica.com/place/Kanem-Bornu.

---. "Mali." *Encyclopedia Britannica*. April 2023. https://www.britannica.com/place/Mali-historical-empire-Africa.

---. "Songhai Empire." *Encyclopedia Britannica*. April 2023. https://www.britannica.com/place/Songhai-empire.

---. "Sonni ʿAlī." *Encyclopedia Britannica*. January 2023. https://www.britannica.com/biography/Sonni-Ali.

Cartwright, Mark. "Ghana Empire." *World History Encyclopedia*. UNESCO Archives. March 2019. https://www.worldhistory.org/Ghana_Empire/.

---. "Kingdom of Abyssinia." *World History Encyclopedia*. UNESCO Archives. April 2019. https://www.worldhistory.org/Kingdom_of_Abyssinia/.

---. "Kingdom of Benin." *World History Encyclopedia*. UNESCO Archives. April 2019. https://www.worldhistory.org/Kingdom_of_Benin/.

---. "Kingdom of Kanem." *World History Encyclopedia*. UNESCO Archives. April 2019. https://www.worldhistory.org/Kingdom_of_Kanem/.

---. "Mali Empire." *World History Encyclopedia*. UNESCO Archives. March 2019. https://www.worldhistory.org/Mali_Empire/.

---. "Mansa Musa I." *World History Encyclopedia*. UNESCO Archives. February 2019. https://www.worldhistory.org/Mansa_Musa_I/.

---. "Songhai Empire." *World History Encyclopedia*. UNESCO Archives. March 2019. https://www.worldhistory.org/Mansa_Musa_I/.

---. "The Spread of Islam in Ancient Africa." *World History Encyclopedia*. UNESCO Archives. May 2019. https://www.worldhistory.org/article/1382/the-spread-of-islam-in-ancient-africa/.

"Church of Saint George." *Brilliant Ethiopia*. Accessed April 2023. https://www.brilliant-ethiopia.com/church-of-saint-george.

"Dawit II." *Wikipedia*. April 2023. https://en.wikipedia.org/wiki/Dawit_II.

Department of the Arts of Africa, Oceania, and the Americas. "Trade and the Spread of Islam in Africa." *Heilbrunn Timeline of Art History*. New York: The Metropolitan Museum of Art. October 2001. http://www.metmuseum.org/toah/hd/tsis/hd_tsis.htm.

Donn, Lin. "Ancient African Kingdom of Ghana." *Mr. Donn's Site for Kids and Teachers*. Accessed April 2023. https://africa.mrdonn.org/ghana.html

"Ethiopian Empire." *New World Encyclopedia*. Accessed April 2023. https://www.newworldencyclopedia.org/entry/Ethiopian_Empire.

Fauvelle, François-Xavier. "Africa's Medieval Golden Age." *History Extra*. Immediate Media Company Limited. July 2020. https://www.historyextra.com/period/what-was-africa-like-middle-ages-medieval-golden-age-culture/.

Foster, Clint. "Africa in the Middle Ages: What Was Medieval African Culture?" *Study.com*. Accessed March 2023. https://study.com/learn/lesson/medieval-africa-history-culture-people.html#:~:text=The%20medieval%20period%20in%20Africa,500%20CE%20to%201500%20CE.

"Ghana Empire Facts for Kids." *Kiddle Encyclopedia*. July 2022. https://kids.kiddle.co/Ghana_Empire.

Graft-Johnson, J. Coleman de. "Mūsā I of Mali." *Encyclopedia Britannica*. October 2022. https://www.britannica.com/biography/Musa-I-of-Mali.

"Idris Alawma." *Encyclopedia Britannica*. Accessed April 2023. https://www.britannica.com/biography/Idris-Alawma.

"Kanem–Bornu Empire Facts for Kids." *Kiddle Encyclopedia*. March 2023. https://kids.kiddle.co/Kanem%E2%80%93Bornu_Empire.

"Mai Idris Alooma." World Eras. *Encyclopedia.com*. April 2023. https://www.encyclopedia.com/history/news-wires-white-papers-and-books/mai-idris-alooma.

"Mali Empire Facts for Kids." Kiddle Encyclopedia. August 2022. https://kids.kiddle.co/Mali_Empire.

"Mansa Musa Facts for Kids." Kiddle Encyclopedia. April 2023. https://kids.kiddle.co/Mansa_Musa.

Maseko, Nomsa. "Timbuktu Manuscripts: Mali's Ancient Documents Captured Online." *BBC*. March 2022. https://www.bbc.com/news/world-africa-60689699.

MasterClass. "Great Mosque of Djenné: History and Architecture of the Djenné Mosque." *MasterClass*. September 2021. https://www.masterclass.com/articles/great-mosque-of-djenne.

"Medieval Africa." *World History with Mrs. Bailey*. Accessed March 2023. https://whbailey.weebly.com/africa-in-the-middle-ages.html.

"Oba Ewuare Ogidigan." World Eras. *Encyclopedia.com*. April 2023. https://www.encyclopedia.com/history/news-wires-white-papers-and-books/oba-ewuare-ogidigan.

Rouch, J. Pierre. "Muḥammad I Askia." *Encyclopedia Britannica*. February 2023. https://www.britannica.com/biography/Muhammad-I-Askia.

Tesfu, Julianna. "Songhai Empire (ca. 1375-1591)." *BlackPast.org*. June 2008. https://www.blackpast.org/global-african-history/songhai-empire-ca-1375-1591/#:~:text=The%20Songhai%20Empire%20was%20the,Northwest%20Nigeria%20and%20central%20Niger.

The British Museum. "The Kingdom of Benin." *Smarthistory*.

"The Djinguereber Mosque." *Abdullatif Al Fozan Award for Mosque Architecture*. Accessed April 2023. https://mosqpedia.org/en/mosque/1101.

"The Expansion of Islam and Trade in Africa." *PBS*. PBS & GBH Educational Foundation. Accessed March 2023. https://myarkansaspbs.pbslearningmedia.org/resource/a12a7d79-ca45-42db-8299-f009a9f3d0a0/the-expansion-of-islam-and-trade-in-africa/.

"The Kingdom of Benin." *National Geographic*. May 2022. https://education.nationalgeographic.org/resource/kingdom-benin/.

Printed in the USA
CPSIA information can be obtained
at www.ICGtesting.com
LVHW022105081223
765524LV00001B/3